MEAL IN A
MUG

You only need a mug and a microwave!

igloobooks

Published in 2015
by Igloo Books Ltd
Cottage Farm
Sywell
NN6 0BJ
www.igloobooks.com

Food photography and recipe development: © Stockfood, The Food Media Agency
Mug cover image © Iain Bagwell / Getty Images
Additional cover images © Thinkstock / Getty Images
Flap images © Stockfood, The Food Media Agency
Additional flap images © Thinkstock / Getty Images

HUN001 0715
2 4 6 8 10 9 7 5 3 1
ISBN 978-1-78440-692-9

Printed and manufactured in China

CONTENTS

MUG OF SOUP

Tomato and Pepper Soup

PREPARATION TIME: 5–10 MINUTES

COOKING TIME: 6–8 MINUTES

Ingredients:

2 tbsp olive oil

600 g / 1 lb 5 oz / 4 cups vine tomatoes, cored and cut into 2 cm (1 in) cubes

1 clove of garlic, minced

½ small onion, finely chopped

1 red pepper, diced

1 tbsp tomato purée

250 ml / 9 fl. oz / 1 cup vegetable stock

a handful of basil leaves

75 g / 3 oz / ⅔ cup crème fraiche

salt and freshly ground black pepper

Method:

1. Combine the oil, tomato, garlic, onion, red pepper, tomato purée, stock and ½ tsp of salt in four large microwaveable mugs.

2. Cover tightly with cling film and microwave on high for 6–8 minutes.

3. Carefully pierce the cling film with a knife to let the steam escape, then remove from the microwave. Blend using a stick blender until the soup is mostly smooth with a little texture.

4. Add half of the basil leaves and pulse a few times to incorporate. Season to taste with salt and pepper.

5. Serve with a dollop of crème fraiche on top and a garnish of the remaining basil.

Tomato and Lentil Soup with Thyme

PREPARATION TIME: 5 MINUTES

COOKING TIME: 8–12 MINUTES

Ingredients:

1 tbsp olive oil

½ clove of garlic, minced

50 g / 1 ¾ oz / ⅓ cup split red lentils, rinsed

625 ml / 1 pints 2 fl. oz / 2 ½ cups vegetable stock

110 g / 4 oz / ½ cup passata

¼ tsp dried thyme

a few sprigs of thyme, leaves stripped and chopped

salt and freshly ground black pepper

Method:

1. Halve the oil and garlic between two microwaveable mugs, then whisk the contents of each mug briefly.

2. Divide the lentils, stock, passata and dried thyme equally between each mug. Add a little seasoning and stir well.

3. Cover each mug with cling film and microwave for 8–10 minutes on a moderate setting, or until the lentils are tender.

4. Carefully remove the mugs from the microwave and pierce the cling film to let the steam escape. Give each mug a stir and check to see if the lentils are tender. If not, microwave for a further 1 ½–2 minutes until soft.

5. Once ready, season to taste and stir through some chopped fresh thyme before serving.

Carrot and Coriander Soup

PREPARATION TIME: 5 MINUTES

COOKING TIME: 8–10 MINUTES

Ingredients:

1 tbsp unsalted butter, melted

½ tbsp sunflower oil

2 large carrots, peeled and grated

¼ tsp caster (superfine) sugar

1 tsp ground coriander

a pinch of ground ginger

375 ml / 13 fl. oz / 1 ½ cups vegetable stock

1 tbsp lemon juice

salt and freshly ground black pepper

Method:

1. Halve the melted butter, oil, carrot, sugar, coriander, ginger and seasoning between two microwaveable mugs, then stir each mug to combine.

2. Top up evenly with the stock, then cover the mugs with cling film and microwave on high for 8–10 minutes, or until the grated carrot is tender.

3. Carefully remove the mugs from the microwave and pierce the cling film with a knife to let the steam escape.

4. Add a little lemon juice to each mug and blend with a stick blender. Season to taste with salt and more freshly ground black pepper before serving.

Carrot Soup with Puff Pastry Straws

PREPARATION TIME: 5 MINUTES

COOKING TIME: 10–12 MINUTES

Ingredients:

2 tbsp unsalted butter, melted

4 large carrots, peeled and grated

1 tsp fresh root ginger, peeled and minced

750 ml / 1 pint 6 fl. oz / 3 cups vegetable stock

1 tbsp lemon juice

2 tbsp Greek yoghurt

a small handful of mint leaves, chopped

8 puff pastry straws, to serve

salt and freshly ground black pepper

Method:

1. Combine the melted butter, carrot, ginger and seasoning between four microwaveable mugs. Top evenly with the stock.

2. Cover the mugs with cling film and microwave on high for 10–12 minutes until the carrots are tender. Carefully remove the mugs from the microwave and pierce the cling film with a knife to let the steam escape.

3. Add a little lemon juice to each mug and blend with a stick blender. Season to taste with salt and pepper. Mix the Greek yoghurt with the mint and spoon on top of the soup, serving with the straws on the side.

Mushroom Soup

PREPARATION TIME: 5–10 MINUTES

COOKING TIME: 6 MINUTES

Ingredients:

2 tbsp olive oil

1 tbsp unsalted butter

1 clove of garlic, minced

300 g / 10 ½ oz / 4 cups mixed wild mushrooms, brushed clean

2 rashers of streaky bacon, chopped

750 ml / 1 pint 6 fl. oz / 3 cups chicken stock

150 ml / 5 fl. oz / ⅔ cup double (heavy) cream

2 tbsp flat-leaf parsley, finely chopped

salt and freshly ground black pepper

Method:

1. Divide the oil, butter, garlic, mushrooms and chopped bacon between four microwaveable mugs.

2. Microwave on high for 1 minute. Carefully remove, stir well, then divide the stock and cream between the mugs.

3. Cover with cling film, poking a few holes in the top. Microwave on medium for 5 minutes, stirring after 2 minutes. Carefully remove from the microwave.

4. Using a teaspoon, carefully remove some of the bacon and mushrooms from each mug and reserve for the garnish.

5. Blend the contents of the mugs until smooth using a stick blender. Season to taste with salt and pepper.

6. Reheat the soups in the microwave if necessary, then top with the reserved bacon, mushrooms and a sprinkling of parsley before serving.

MAKES 4 MUGS

Chunky Vegetable Soup

PREPARATION TIME: 10 MINUTES

COOKING TIME: 5 MINUTES

Ingredients:

1 tbsp olive oil

½ small onion, chopped

½ small red onion, chopped

1 clove of garlic, minced

200 g / 7 oz / 1 cup canned chopped tomatoes

375 ml / 13 fl. oz / 1 ½ cup vegetable stock

¼ white baguette, sliced

a small bunch of basil, leaves picked

salt and freshly ground black pepper

Method:

1. Divide the oil, onions and garlic between two microwaveable mugs. Cook on high for 1 ½–2 minutes and carefully remove from the microwave.

2. Divide the chopped tomatoes between each mug and top up with stock. Add a little seasoning, stir well and return to the microwave, cooking for a further 2 ½–3 minutes, or until the soup is piping hot.

3. Adjust the seasoning to taste and leave to stand, covered loosely, for a few minutes as you prepare the garnish.

4. Toast the slices of baguette in a toaster or under a hot grill. Serve them with the soup, topped with a garnish of basil leaves.

Pea and Cheddar Soup

PREPARATION TIME: 5–10 MINUTES

COOKING TIME: 6 ½ MINUTES

Ingredients:

2 tbsp unsalted butter

1 small onion, finely chopped

4 rashers streaky bacon, chopped

350 g / 12 oz / 3 cups fresh peas

500 ml / 18 fl. oz / 2 cups vegetable stock

250 ml / 9 fl. oz / 1 cup whole milk

110 g / 4 oz / 1 cup Cheddar, grated

salt and freshly ground black pepper

Method:

1. Divide the butter, onion and chopped bacon between four microwaveable mugs. Cook on high for 1 minute and then remove carefully from the microwave.

2. Divide the peas, stock and milk between each mug. Return to the microwave for an additional 5 minutes, stirring halfway through cooking. Carefully remove from the microwave.

3. Remove a few pieces of bacon from each mug and reserve for the garnish. Divide most of the Cheddar between each mug and blend until smooth with a stick blender. Season to taste.

4. Briefly reheat the soups for 30 seconds in the microwave if necessary, before topping with the remaining Cheddar and reserved bacon to serve.

Pumpkin Soup

PREPARATION TIME: 5–10 MINUTES

COOKING TIME: 10 MINUTES

Ingredients:

1 tbsp onion, chopped

½ tsp of garlic, chopped

150 g / 5 ¼ oz / ⅔ cup pumpkin, peeled and cut into 1 cm (½ in) cubes

a pinch of curry powder

125 ml / 4 ½ fl. oz / ½ cup vegetable stock

60 ml / 2 fl. oz / ¼ cup whole milk

salt and freshly ground black pepper

Method:

1. Combine the onion, garlic and pumpkin in a large microwaveable mugs. Cover with cling film and cook on high for 3–4 minutes until the pumpkin is tender.

2. Carefully remove from the microwave and add the curry powder, stock, milk and some seasoning.

3. Return to the microwave and cook on high for a further 3–5 minutes, stirring after 2 minutes, until the pumpkin is very soft.

4. Carefully remove the mug from the microwave and blend with a stick blender. Season to taste with salt and pepper before serving.

cauliflower Soup

PREPARATION TIME: 5 MINUTES

COOKING TIME: 6–7 MINUTES

Ingredients:

1 tbsp olive oil

1 tbsp onion, finely chopped

1 carrot, peeled and chopped

½ small head cauliflower, prepared into small florets

375 ml / 13 fl. oz / 1 ½ cups vegetable stock

1 tbsp tomato purée

a small bunch of flat-leaf parsley, torn

salt and freshly ground black pepper

Method:

1. Divide the oil and onion between two microwaveable mugs. Microwave on high for 1–1 ½ minutes.

2. Add the carrot and cauliflower to each mug, covering them with cling film. Cook on high for 2 minutes.

3. Carefully remove the mugs from the microwave and pierce the cling film with a knife to let the steam escape. Remove the cling film and add the stock and tomato purée, stirring thoroughly.

4. Return to the microwave and cook on high for a further 3 ½ minutes, stirring halfway through, until the broth is hot.

5. Carefully remove the mugs from the microwave and season to taste with salt and pepper. Serve with a garnish of parsley on top.

Spinach and Rocket Soup

PREPARATION TIME: 10 MINUTES

COOKING TIME: 6–8 MINUTES

Ingredients:

1 tbsp sunflower oil

½ clove of garlic, minced

½ onion, finely chopped

½ large white potato, peeled and diced

250 ml / 9 fl. oz / 1 cups vegetable stock

50 g / 1 ¾ oz / 1 cups baby spinach, washed

50 g / 1 ¾ oz / 1 cups rocket (arugula), washed

110 ml / 4 fl. oz / ½ cup whole milk

1 tbsp Roquefort, cubed

salt and freshly ground black pepper

Method:

1. Divide the oil, garlic and onion between two large microwaveable mugs. Cook on high for 1–1 ½ minutes.

2. Remove from the microwave and divide the potato, stock and a little seasoning between each mug. Return to the microwave and cook on high for 4–6 minutes, stirring after 2 minutes, until the potato is tender.

3. Carefully remove the mugs from the microwave and divide the spinach and most of the rocket between each mug, stirring well.

4. Add the milk to each mug and blend with a stick blender until smooth. Reheat the soups in the microwave for 30 seconds if necessary.

5. Season to taste with salt and pepper. Serve with a garnish of Roquefort and the remaining rocket leaves on top.

Quinoa and Sweetcorn Soup

PREPARATION TIME: 10 MINUTES

COOKING TIME: 10 MINUTES

Ingredients:

2 tbsp olive oil

2 medium white potatoes, peeled and diced

1 red pepper, finely diced

150 g / 5 oz / 1 ½ cups green (string) beans, trimmed and diced

200 g / 7 oz / 1 cup canned sweetcorn

175 g / 6 oz / 1 cup quinoa, rinsed in cold water

1000 ml / 1 pint 16 fl. oz / 4 cups vegetable stock

salt and freshly ground black pepper

Method:

1. Divide the oil and potato between four large microwaveable mugs, toss with plenty of seasoning and cook on high for 4 minutes.

2. Carefully remove the mugs and divide the pepper, beans, sweetcorn, quinoa and stock between each mug, stirring well. Cover the mugs loosely with cling film and microwave for a further 6 minutes, stirring after 3 minutes.

3. Remove the mugs from the microwave and leave them to stand, covered, for 5 minutes.

4. Remove the cling film and adjust the seasoning to taste before serving.

MAKES
4
MUGS

MAKES 2 MUGS

Indian Chicken Soup

PREPARATION TIME: 10 MINUTES

COOKING TIME: 5–7 MINUTES

Ingredients:

1 tbsp sunflower oil

1 tbsp mild curry paste

1 large skinless chicken breast, diced

1 carrot, peeled and diced

1 stick of celery, peeled and finely sliced

½ onion, diced

375 ml / 13 fl. oz / 1 ½ cups chicken stock

110 g / 4 oz / ½ cup passata

1 tbsp coriander (cilantro), chopped

salt and freshly ground black pepper

Method:

1. Divide the sunflower oil and curry paste between two microwaveable mugs, whisking to combine.

2. Divide the chicken between the mugs and stir well to coat in the mixture, then season with salt and pepper. Cook in the microwave on high for 2 minutes.

3. Carefully remove from the microwave and add the carrot, celery, onion, stock, passata and seasoning. Stir well and cover loosely with cling film.

4. Microwave on high for 3–5 minutes, stirring halfway through, until the vegetables are tender and the chicken is cooked through.

5. Carefully remove the mugs from the microwave and leave them to stand briefly before discarding the cling film.

6. Season the soup with salt and pepper before garnishing with chopped coriander and serving.

clam chowder

PREPARATION TIME: 10 MINUTES

COOKING TIME: 10 MINUTES

Ingredients:

2 tbsp butter

2 medium floury potatoes, peeled and diced

½ onion, finely diced

2 rashers of bacon, chopped

2 tbsp plain (all-purpose) flour

600 ml / 1 pint 2 fl. oz / 2 ½ cups whole milk

110 ml / 4 fl. oz / ½ cup double (heavy) cream

a pinch of dried parsley

350 g / 12 oz / 2 cups canned clams, drained

oyster crackers, to serve

salt and freshly ground black pepper

Method:

1. Divide the butter, potatoes, onion and bacon between four large microwaveable mugs, then cover tightly with cling film.

2. Microwave on high for 5–7 minutes, stirring carefully after 3 minutes, until the potatoes are tender.

3. Whisk together the flour with 75 ml / 3 fl. oz / ⅓ cup of the milk in a small bowl. Divide the mixture between the mugs and top each up with the remaining milk and the cream.

4. Add the parsley, clams and seasoning to each mug, stirring well. Cover the mugs again with cling film and microwave on medium for 3 minutes, stirring once.

5. Remove the mugs from the microwave and blend with a stick blender until smooth. Adjust the seasoning to taste and serve with the oyster crackers on top.

Haddock Soup

PREPARATION TIME: 10 MINUTES

COOKING TIME: 6–8 MINUTES

Ingredients:

2 tbsp unsalted butter

a pinch of ground turmeric

1 tsp Madras curry powder

a pinch of ground cumin

½ medium floury potato, peeled and diced

175 g / 6 oz / 1 ¼ cups dyed skinless haddock fillet, diced

375 ml / 13 fl. oz / 1 ½ cups whole milk

1 tbsp double (heavy) cream

a few chive stalks, snipped

salt and freshly ground black pepper

Method:

1. Divide the butter between two microwaveable mugs. Cook on high for 30 seconds or until melted.

2. Divide the ground spices between the mugs, stirring into the melted butter. Return to the microwave and cook on high for 5 seconds.

3. Remove from the microwave and divide the potato and haddock between the mugs. Top up with the milk, stirring well.

4. Return to the microwave, cover and cook on high for 4–6 minutes, or until the fish is cooked through and the potato is tender.

5. Carefully remove the mugs from the microwave and reserve 1 tbsp of the cooked haddock from each mug for a garnish. Use a stick blender to purée the soups in the mugs, then season them to taste.

6. Serve with the reserved haddock, a drizzle of cream, and some chopped chives on top.

MAIN MEAL MUGS

Beef Pot Pie

PREPARATION TIME: 15 MINUTES

COOKING TIME: 30–40 MINUTES

Ingredients:

2 tbsp butter, cubed

2 large carrots, peeled and diced

1 onion, finely chopped

500 ml / 18 fl. oz / 2 cups beef stock

600 g / 1 lb 5 oz / 4 cups cooked roast beef, cut
    into chunks

110 g / 4 oz ready-made shortcrust pastry

1 small egg, beaten with 1 tbsp water

salt and freshly ground black pepper

Method:

1. Divide the butter, carrots, onion and stock between
   the mugs. Season with salt and pepper and cover with
   cling film.

2. Microwave on medium for 6–8 minutes, stirring from
   time to time. Remove from the microwave and divide
   the cooked beef between the mugs. Cook for a further
   2–4 minutes, then remove and leave to one side. If you
   don't want a pastry lid on your pie, season and ensure
   the beef is piping hot before serving.

3. Preheat the oven to 180°C (160°C fan) / 350F / gas 4.
   Roll out the pastry on a lightly floured surface to 1 cm
   (½ in) thickness. Cut out four rounds to act as lids for
   the mugs.

4. Brush the rim of the mugs with a little egg wash, then
   drape the pastry rounds on top and seal against the
   rims with the tines of a fork. Bore a hole in the centre
   and brush with more egg wash.

5. Place on a baking tray and bake for 20–25 minutes
   until golden before serving.

Beef Goulash with Sour Cream

PREPARATION TIME: 10 MINUTES

COOKING TIME: 12–16 MINUTES

Ingredients:

600 g / 1 lb 5 oz / 4 cups cooked roast beef, cut into chunks

1 small onion, chopped

2 cloves of garlic, minced

1 stick of celery, finely diced

1 tsp caster (superfine) sugar

2 tsp paprika

a pinch of dried oregano

225 g / 8 oz / 1 cup passata

500 ml / 18 fl. oz / 2 cups beef stock

110 g / 4 oz / ½ cup sour cream, to serve

salt and freshly ground black pepper

Method:

1. Divide all of the ingredients except the beef and sour cream between four large microwaveable mugs and season. Cover tightly with cling film and microwave for 8–10 minutes, stirring well throughout.

2. Add the cooked beef and cover again, then cook for a further 4–6 minutes until the beef is piping hot.

3. Season to taste with salt and pepper before serving with sour cream on top.

41

Chilli Con Carne

PREPARATION TIME: 10 MINUTES

COOKING TIME: 15 MINUTES

Ingredients:

225 g / 8 oz / 1 ½ cups beef mince

½ small onion, chopped

1 clove of garlic, minced

200 g / 17 oz / 1 cup canned chopped tomatoes

150 g / 5 oz / ¾ cup canned kidney beans

½ tsp chilli (chili) powder

a pinch of ground cumin

lime wedges, to serve

tortilla chips, to serve

salt and freshly ground black pepper

Method:

1. Season the beef and divide between two large microwaveable mugs. Cook on high for 3–5 minutes, or until the beef mince is browning. Stir to break up the mince.

2. Carefully remove from the microwave and divide the remaining ingredients apart from the lime wedges and tortilla chips between the mugs.

3. Stir well, cover with cling film and cook on medium for 8–10 minutes, stirring halfway through cooking.

4. Carefully remove from the microwave and leave to stand for a few minutes before seasoning to taste. Serve with tortilla chips and lime wedges on the side.

Lentil Thyme Stew with Sausage

PREPARATION TIME: 10 MINUTES

COOKING TIME: 6–10 MINUTES

Ingredients:

1 tsp olive oil

½ stick of celery, finely diced

1 tbsp onion, finely diced

a pinch of dried thyme

50 g / 1 ½ oz / ¼ cup green lentils

50 g / 1 ½ oz / ¼ cup canned chopped tomatoes

175 ml / 6 fl. oz / ¾ cup vegetable stock

60 g / 2 oz / ½ cup cooked smoked sausage

a few sprigs of thyme, to garnish

salt and freshly ground black pepper

Method:

1. Add the oil to a large microwaveable mug, then add the celery, onion, thyme and a little salt and pepper.

2. Microwave on high for 1 minute. Carefully remove from the microwave and add the lentils, chopped tomatoes and stock, stirring well.

3. Cover with cling film and microwave on medium for 4–6 minutes until the lentils are tender. Microwave for a further minute if not ready, topping up with water if needed.

4. Carefully remove from the microwave and leave to stand for a few minutes. Remove the cling film, stir well and season to taste with salt and pepper.

5. Pierce the cooked sausage in several places with a knife. Microwave on high for 1 minute until piping hot, then slice and serve on top of the lentils, garnished with thyme.

Mushroom and Bacon Pasta

PREPARATION TIME: 10 MINUTES

COOKING TIME: 15–20 MINUTES

Ingredients:

2 tbsp butter

1 clove of garlic, chopped

150 g / 5 oz / 1 cup bacon lardons

150 g / 5 oz / 2 cups button mushrooms, sliced

350 g / 12 oz / 3 cups penne pasta

75 ml / 3 fl. oz / ⅓ cup double (heavy) cream

55 g / 2 oz / ½ cup Parmesan, finely grated

salt and freshly ground black pepper

Method:

1. Divide the butter, garlic, bacon and mushrooms between four large microwaveable mugs. Cook on high in the microwave for 3–5 minutes, stirring after 2 minutes.

2. Divide the pasta between the mugs and pour in enough water to cover them by 2 cm (1 in).

3. Microwave the pasta on high for 10–12 minutes until 'al dente', stirring occasionally. Cook for an additional 1–2 minutes if not ready.

4. Divide the cream into the mugs, stir well and season with salt and pepper. Heat for a further minute if necessary, then garnish with Parmesan before serving.

MAKES
4
MUGS

MAKES
4
MUGS

Macaroni Cheese with Pulled Pork

PREPARATION TIME: 10 MINUTES

COOKING TIME: 8–10 MINUTES

Ingredients:

250 g / 9 oz / 2 cups elbow macaroni

500 ml / 18 fl. oz / 2 cups whole milk

110 g / 4 oz / 1 cup Cheddar, finely grated

350 g / 12 oz cooked pork ribs, trimmed

salt and freshly ground black pepper

Method:

1. Divide the macaroni and milk between four large microwaveable mugs.

2. Place the mugs on a plate and microwave for 3–4 minutes, stirring every minute until the macaroni is tender. Continue to microwave in 1-minute bursts if not ready.

3. Carefully remove from the microwave and stir in the Cheddar, seasoning to taste.

4. Pull apart the pork ribs and stir into the pasta. Cook in the microwave for a further 2–4 minutes, or until the Cheddar is melted and the pork is piping hot.

chicken Noodles

PREPARATION TIME: 10 MINUTES

COOKING TIME: 6 MINUTES

Ingredients:

2 tbsp sunflower oil

1 onion, finely chopped

2 carrots, peeled and finely diced

2 sticks of celery, finely sliced

800 ml / 1 pint 9 fl. oz / 3 ½ cups chicken stock

225 g / 8 oz / 2 cups cooked udon noodles

350 g / 12 oz / 2 ⅓ cups cooked chicken breast, roughly chopped

1 tbsp flat-leaf parsley, chopped

salt and freshly ground black pepper

Method:

1. Divide the oil, onion, carrot and celery between four microwaveable mugs. Season with salt and pepper and microwave on high for 2 minutes, stirring after 1 minute.

2. Carefully remove from the microwave and divide the stock, noodles, chicken and parsley between the mugs. Stir briefly and cover with cling film, poking a few holes.

3. Microwave on medium for 4 minutes, stirring after 2 minutes.

4. Carefully remove from the microwave and season to taste before serving.

MAKES
2
MUGS

chicken Pie

PREPARATION TIME: 15 MINUTES

COOKING TIME: 25–30 MINUTES

Ingredients:

1 tbsp butter

1 tbsp plain (all-purpose) flour, plus extra for dusting

250 ml / 9 fl. oz / 1 cup whole milk

¼ small leek, finely sliced

2 cooked chicken thighs, diced

a small handful of sage leaves

55 g / 2 oz ready-made puff pastry

½ small egg, beaten with 1 tbsp of water

salt and freshly ground black pepper

Method:

1. Place the butter in a microwaveable jug and microwave on high for 20–30 seconds until melted. Remove from the microwave and whisk in the flour until you have a roux.

2. Slowly whisk in the milk, then microwave on high for 1 ½ minutes. Carefully remove, stir in the leek and microwave for a further 1 ½–2 minutes until thickened.

3. Stir the chicken and sage leaves into the sauce. Adjust the seasoning to taste and divide the filling between two microwaveable mugs.

4. Preheat the oven to 200°C (180°C fan) / 400F / gas 6. Roll out the pastry on a lightly floured surface into a round approximately 5 mm (¼ in) thick and cut out two rounds to act as lids.

5. Brush the rims of the mugs with the egg wash, then drape the pastry rounds over the mugs and seal well against the outside of the mugs. Brush the tops with more egg wash and bore a small hole in their centres.

6. Bake for 18–22 minutes until golden brown and puffed before serving.

53

Prawn and Pea Pies

PREPARATION TIME: 5–10 MINUTES

COOKING TIME: 6–7 MINUTES

Ingredients:

1 tbsp butter

2 tbsp plain (all-purpose) flour

600 ml / 1 pint 2 fl. oz / 2 ½ cups whole milk

250 g / 9 oz / 2 cups petit pois

450 g / 1 lb / 3 cups peeled prawns (shrimps), deveined with tails intact

600 g / 1 lb 5 oz / 4 cups cooked mashed potato, warmed

75 g / 3 oz / ¾ cup Parmesan, finely grated

salt and freshly ground black pepper

Method:

1. Divide the butter between four microwaveable mugs. Microwave on high for 10–15 seconds until melted.

2. Divide the flour evenly between the mugs and whisk well. Whisk 150 ml / ¼ pint / ⅔ cup of milk slowly into each mug until smooth, then microwave on high for 2 minutes.

3. Add the peas, prawns and a little seasoning, stir well and microwave for a further 3 minutes.

4. Remove from the microwave and top with the mashed potato and then the Parmesan. Microwave on high for a further minute until golden on top and the mashed potato is warmed through.

MAKES
4
MUGS

Prawn, Noodle and Mushroom Stew

PREPARATION TIME: 10 MINUTES

COOKING TIME: 5 MINUTES

Ingredients:

125 g / 4 ½ oz / 1 cup fine egg noodles

500 ml / 18 fl. oz / 2 cups chicken stock, hot

½ yellow pepper, finely diced

½ spring onion (scallion), finely sliced

225 g / 8 oz / 1 ½ cups peeled prawns (shrimps), deveined

a small handful of dried shiitake mushrooms

dark soy sauce, to taste

½ lime, juiced

freshly ground black pepper

Method:

1. Divide the egg noodles between two large microwaveable mugs. Divide the stock between the mugs and microwave on high for 1 ½ minutes.

2. Carefully remove from the microwave and stir gently. Add the yellow pepper, spring onion, prawns and mushrooms, then stir again.

3. Microwave on medium for 3–4 minutes until the prawns are pink and tender to the touch.

4. Season to taste with soy sauce, lime juice and pepper before serving.

Paella

PREPARATION TIME: 10 MINUTES

COOKING TIME: 25–30 MINUTES

Ingredients:

2 tbsp olive oil

1 red onion, chopped

1 red pepper, diced

2 cloves of garlic, minced

2 slices of thick-cut ham, chopped

150 g / 5 oz / 1 cup short-grain rice, rinsed

500 ml / 18 fl. oz / 2 cups chicken stock, hot

a few strands of saffron, infused in the stock

1 tsp paprika

2 large skinless chicken thighs, diced

300 g / 10 ½ oz / 2 cups peeled prawns (shrimps), deveined

a small handful of flat-leaf parsley, sliced

salt and freshly ground black pepper

Method:

1. Divide the oil, onion, pepper, garlic and ham between four large microwaveable mugs. Microwave on high for 2 minutes.

2. Divide the rice, infused stock, and paprika between the mugs, stirring well. Cover with cling film and microwave on high for 8–10 minutes. Stir well, and microwave on medium for a further 4 minutes.

3. Carefully remove the mugs from the microwave, carefully peeling away the cling film. Stir gently, then add the chicken.

4. Return the mugs to the microwave and cook on high for a further 4 minutes. Add the prawns and cook for 6 minutes.

5. Remove from the microwave and leave to stand, covered, for 5 minutes. Season to taste and garnish with parsley before serving.

MAKES
2
MUGS

Bean and Vegetable Stew

PREPARATION TIME: 10 MINUTES

COOKING TIME: 10 MINUTES

Ingredients:

1 tbsp olive oil

1 carrot peeled and finely diced

½ courgette (zucchini), finely diced

1 stick of celery, finely diced

½ onion, finely chopped

250 ml / 9 fl. oz / 1 cup vegetable stock

200 g / 7 oz / 1 cup canned chopped tomatoes

200 g / 7 oz / 1 cup canned cannellini beans, drained

1 tbsp Parmesan, grated

salt and freshly ground black pepper

Method:

1. Divide the oil and vegetables between two large microwaveable mugs. Cook on high for 2 minutes, stirring after 1 minute.

2. Carefully remove from the microwave and divide the stock, chopped tomatoes and beans between the mugs.

3. Stir well and cover with cling film, poking a few holes. Microwave on high for 6–8 minutes until the beans are tender.

4. Carefully remove from the microwave and leave to stand, covered, for 2 minutes. Remove the cling film, stir well and season to taste with salt and pepper.

5. Serve with a garnish of Parmesan on top.

Spiral Pasta and Cheese

PREPARATION TIME: 5 MINUTES

COOKING TIME: 5–6 MINUTES

Ingredients:

75 g / 2 ½ oz / ¾ cup fusilli pasta

1 tsp olive oil

1 tbsp Parmesan, finely grated

1 tsp breadcrumbs, toasted

a pinch of dried thyme

salt and freshly ground black pepper

Method:

1. Add the pasta to a large microwaveable mug and cover with at least 2 cm (1 in) of water.

2. Place the mug on a flat microwaveable plate and microwave on high for 3–5 minutes, stirring at 1-minute intervals, until 'al dente'. Continue to microwave for a further minute if not ready.

3. Carefully remove from the microwave and drain the pasta if needed, then toss with the olive oil.

4. Top with a mixture of the Parmesan, breadcrumbs and thyme before serving.

Cheese and Vegetable Pie

PREPARATION TIME: 10 MINUTES

COOKING TIME: 20–25 MINUTES

Ingredients:

2 tbsp butter

1 small head of broccoli, prepared into small florets

1 small head of cauliflower, prepared into small florets

100 g / 3 ½ oz / 1 cup Red Leicester (or similar), cubed

110 g / 4 oz ready-made puff pastry

a little plain (all-purpose) flour, for dusting

1 small egg, beaten with 1 tbsp water

1 tsp white sesame seeds

1 tsp black sesame seeds

salt and freshly ground black pepper

Method:

1. Preheat the oven to 190°C (170°C fan) / 375F / gas 5. Divide the butter, broccoli and cauliflower between four large microwaveable mugs. Cover with cling film and microwave on high for 5 minutes.

2. Carefully remove the mugs and stir in the cheese and seasoning to taste. Roll out the pastry on a lightly floured surface into a round approximately ½ cm (¼ in) thick.

3. Cut out four rounds of pastry to act as lids for the pies. Brush the rims of the mugs with a little egg wash and drape over the pastry.

4. Seal well against the rims and brush the tops of the pastry with more egg wash. Sprinkle over the sesame seeds and arrange the mugs on a baking tray.

5. Bake for 15–18 minutes until puffed and golden on top before serving.

Cheese Soufflé

PREPARATION TIME: 10 MINUTES

COOKING TIME: 20–25 MINUTES

Ingredients:

55 g / 2 oz / ⅓ cup plain (all-purpose) flour, sifted

a pinch of mustard powder

a pinch of paprika

400 g / 14 oz / 2 cups evaporated milk

2 tbsp butter, softened

225 g / 8 oz / 2 cups Cheddar, grated

6 medium eggs, separated

1 tsp cream of tartar

salt and freshly ground black pepper

Method:

1. Divide the flour, mustard powder, paprika, evaporated milk, butter and a little seasoning between four large microwaveable mugs. Stir well until smooth.

2. Microwave on medium for 4 minutes, stirring after 2 minutes, until thickened. Carefully remove from the microwave.

3. Divide the cheese between the mugs, stir well and microwave on high for 2 minutes. Carefully remove to one side and scrape into a bowl.

4. Beat the egg yolks in a separate bowl until pale and thick. Beat the egg whites with the cream of tartar in another clean bowl until stiffly peaked.

5. Pour the cheese mixture over the egg yolks, folding to incorporate. Fold into the egg whites until just combined. Divide the mixture between the mugs and run the tip of your thumb around the insides of the rims.

6. Microwave on low for 10 minutes. Rotate the mugs and microwave on medium for a further 6–8 minutes until risen and golden on top. Serve immediately.

spaghetti squash Noodles

PREPARATION TIME: 10 MINUTES

COOKING TIME: 5 MINUTES

Ingredients:

110 g / 4 oz / ½ cup peanut butter

2 tbsp dark soy sauce

2 tbsp lime juice

1 tbsp light brown sugar

1 tbsp sesame oil

1 spaghetti squash, halved and peeled, with seeds removed

2 carrots, peeled and julienned

2 spring onions (scallions), finely sliced

2 tbsp peanuts, crushed

a small handful of coriander (cilantro), to garnish

Method:

1. Divide the peanut butter, soy sauce, lime juice, sugar, sesame oil and 2 tbsp of warm water between four microwaveable mugs. Microwave on high for 1 minute, and then remove and stir well.

2. Cut the squash into portions and pass through a spiralizer, collecting the strands in a bowl of cold water. If you don't own a spiralizer, you can julienne the squash instead.

3. Rinse the squash well, then drain and pat dry. Divide between the mugs and toss with the peanut sauce. Cover the mugs with cling film and cook on high in the microwave for 3–4 minutes.

4. Carefully remove from the microwave and leave to stand briefly before removing the cling film. Stir briefly before garnishing with the carrots, spring onion, peanuts and coriander.

Vegetable and Buckwheat Bakes

PREPARATION TIME: 10 MINUTES

COOKING TIME: 10–15 MINUTES

Ingredients:

1 tbsp sunflower oil

85 g / 3 oz / ½ cup buckwheat

250 ml / 9 fl. oz / 1 cup vegetable stock

½ leek, sliced

½ large floury potato, peeled and diced

75 g / 2 ½ oz / 1 cup button mushrooms, sliced

1 carrot, peeled and grated

110 g / 4 oz / 1 cup Cheddar, grated

1 tbsp flat-leaf parsley, finely chopped

salt and freshly ground black pepper

Method:

1. Divide the oil, buckwheat and stock between two large microwaveable mugs. Cover with cling film and cook on medium for 6–8 minutes.

2. Carefully remove from the microwave and leave to stand, covered, for 5 minutes. Remove the cling film and fluff with a fork.

3. Divide the leek, potato and mushrooms between two separate mugs. Season with salt and pepper and microwave on high for 3–4 minutes, stirring after 2 minutes.

4. Remove from the microwave and divide between the mugs of buckwheat. Add the carrot and half the cheese, seasoning to taste with salt and pepper.

5. Divide between the mugs and top with the rest of the cheese and the parsley. Microwave on high for 1 ½–2 minutes until the cheese has melted.

MAKES
2
MUGS

Spinach Ravioli

PREPARATION TIME: 10 MINUTES

COOKING TIME: 5 MINUTES

Ingredients:

non-stick cooking spray

150 g / 5 oz / 1 ½ cups Parmesan, grated

2 tbsp olive oil

1 spring onion (scallion), sliced

225 g / 8 oz / 2 cups ready-made small ravioli

750 ml / 1 pint 6 fl. oz / 3 cups vegetable stock

100 g / 3 ½ oz / 2 cups baby spinach, washed and chopped

salt and freshly ground black pepper

Method:

1. Spray a microwaveable plate with non-stick cooking spray. Pile small mounds of the grated Parmesan onto the plate, saving a couple of tablespoons as a garnish.

2. Microwave the Parmesan on high in 10-second bursts until melted and golden. Carefully remove to one side to cool. These will form the Parmesan crisps to garnish.

3. Divide the olive oil, spring onion, ravioli and stock between four microwaveable mugs. Cover with cling film and microwave on high for 2–3 minutes until the stock is piping hot.

4. Carefully remove from the microwave and season to taste. Garnish the mugs with the chopped spinach, remaining grated Parmesan and Parmesan crisps.

Sticky Lemon Rice

PREPARATION TIME: 10 MINUTES

COOKING TIME: 10–15 MINUTES

Ingredients:

1 tbsp butter

½ onion, finely chopped

½ lemon, juiced and zested

110 g / 4 oz / ¾ cup long-grain white rice, rinsed

375 ml / 13 fl. oz / 1 ½ cups vegetable stock

a small handful of basil, chopped

salt and freshly ground black pepper

Method:

1. Divide the butter and onion between two large microwaveable mugs. Microwave on high for 1 ½ minutes, then carefully remove.

2. Divide the lemon juice and zest, rice and stock between the mugs. Stir well and microwave on high for 8–10 minutes until the rice is tender. Cook for a further 1 ½–2 minutes if not ready.

3. Carefully remove from the microwave and stir in the basil. Season to taste before serving.

MAKES 2 MUGS

MAKES
4
MUGS

Bread Salad with Feta

PREPARATION TIME: 10 MINUTES

COOKING TIME: 5 MINUTES

Ingredients:

1 small baguette, sliced

75 ml / 3 fl. oz / ⅓ cup olive oil

110 ml / 4 fl. oz / ½ cup extra-virgin olive oil

3 tbsp balsamic vinegar

½ tsp caster (superfine) sugar

2 spring onions (scallions)

2 little gem lettuce, halved

a small handful of rocket (arugula)

a few mint leaves

225 g / 8 oz / 1 ½ cups cherry tomatoes, halved

150 g / 5 oz / 1 ½ cups feta, cubed

salt and freshly ground black pepper

Method:

1. Brush the slices of baguette with olive oil on both sides. Toast under a hot grill for a minute on both sides until golden. Remove to a wire rack to cool.

2. Whisk together the extra-virgin olive oil, balsamic vinegar, sugar and seasoning in a mug or small bowl.

3. Finely slice the whites of the spring onions and set to one side. Finely chop the green stalks and stir into the dressing.

4. Arrange the lettuce, rocket, mint leaves, whites of the spring onions, tomatoes and feta in four mugs. Tuck the toasted baguette slices into the mugs alongside the salads.

5. Spoon the dressing over the salads before serving.

DESSERT MUGS

Smooth Chocolate Mousse

PREPARATION TIME: 10 MINUTES

COOKING TIME: 2 MINUTES   **CHILLING TIME:** 2 HOURS

Ingredients:

250 g / 9 oz / 1 ⅔ cups dark chocolate, chopped

350 ml / 12 fl. oz / 1 ½ cups double (heavy) cream

100 g / 3 ½ oz / 4 cups white marshmallows

2 tbsp cocoa powder

Method:

1. Combine the chocolate with 100 ml / 3 ½ fl. oz / ½ cup of the cream and the marshmallows in a large microwaveable bowl.

2. Microwave on high for 2 minutes, stirring after 1 minute, until melted. Remove from the microwave and stir until fully incorporated. Leave to cool slightly.

3. Whip the remaining cream in a separate bowl until softly peaked. Fold one-third into the melted chocolate mixture, then stir in the remaining cream.

4. Spoon into mugs, spread the tops smooth with a wet tablespoon and cover with cling film. Chill for 2 hours.

5. Dust with cocoa powder before serving.

Chocolate Orange Pudding Cups

PREPARATION TIME: 10 MINUTES

COOKING TIME: 2–3 MINUTES   **CHILLING TIME:** 4 HOURS

Ingredients:

55 g / 2 oz / ¼ cup caster (superfine) sugar

1 tbsp cornflour (cornstarch)

a pinch of salt

250 ml / 9 fl. oz / 1 cup whole milk

1 large egg yolk

110 g / 4 oz / ¾ cup dark chocolate chips

1 tbsp unsalted butter

1 tbsp orange liqueur

1 tsp orange zest, grated

1 tsp cocoa powder

1 tsp dark chocolate, grated

Method:

1. Divide the sugar, cornflour and salt between two microwaveable mugs. Divide half of the milk and the egg yolk between the mugs and whisk until smooth, then whisk in the remaining milk.

2. Heat in the microwave on medium for 2–3 minutes, stirring after 1 ½ minutes, until thickened.

3. Carefully remove from the microwave and leave to stand for 1 minute. Whisk in the chocolate chips, butter, orange liqueur and zest until smooth and fully incorporated.

4. Cover with cling film and chill for 4 hours. Garnish with a dusting of cocoa powder and a sprinkling of grated chocolate when ready to serve.

Chocolate and Raspberry Pudding

PREPARATION TIME: 10 MINUTES

COOKING TIME: 2 MINUTES   **CHILLING TIME:** 2 HOURS

Ingredients:

250 g / 9 oz / 1 2/3 cups dark chocolate, chopped

350 ml / 12 fl. oz / 1 ½ cups double (heavy) cream

100 g / 3 ½ oz / 4 cups white marshmallows

1 tbsp cocoa powder

2 tbsp framboise liqueur

8 raspberries

2 tbsp lemon juice

2 tbsp granulated sugar

Method:

1. Combine the chocolate with 100 ml / 3 ½ fl. oz / ½ cup of the cream and the marshmallows in a large microwaveable bowl.

2. Microwave on high for 2 minutes, stirring after 1 minute, until melted. Remove from the microwave and add the cocoa powder and framboise, stirring until fully incorporated. Leave to cool slightly.

3. Whip the remaining cream in a separate bowl until softly peaked. Fold one-third into the melted chocolate mixture and then incorporate the remaining cream.

4. Spoon into mugs, spread the tops smooth with a wet tablespoon and cover with cling film. Chill for 2 hours.

5. Toss the raspberries with the lemon juice and then the granulated sugar before using to garnish the puddings.

Apple Pie

PREPARATION TIME: 10 MINUTES

COOKING TIME: 20–25 MINUTES

Ingredients:

600 g / 1 lb 5 oz / 4 cups Bramley apples, peeled, cored, and diced

75 g / 3 oz / ⅓ cup caster (superfine) sugar

½ lemon, juiced

2 tbsp water

4 sheets of ready-made filo pastry, kept under a damp cloth

2 tbsp unsalted butter, melted

½ tsp ground cinnamon

custard, to serve

Method:

1. Preheat the oven to 190°C (170°C fan) / 375F / gas 5.

2. Divide the apples, sugar, lemon juice and water between four microwaveable mugs, tossing the ingredients together.

3. Cover with cling film and cook in the microwave on high for 4 minutes, stirring after 2 minutes, until softened.

4. Carefully remove from the microwave and stir again. Scrunch up the sheets of pastry, fitting them to size inside the cups on top of the apple.

5. Sit the cups on a baking tray and top with the melted butter and a pinch of cinnamon. Bake for 15–18 minutes until golden brown on top.

6. Remove from the oven and leave to cool slightly before serving with the custard.

MAKES
4
MUGS

Fig and Raspberry Crumble

PREPARATION TIME: 10 MINUTES

COOKING TIME: 3 MINUTES

Ingredients:

75 g / 2 ½ oz / ½ cup plain (all-purpose) flour

75 g / 2 ½ oz / ¼ cup unsalted butter, cubed

60 g / 2 ¼ oz / ⅓ cup soft light brown sugar

a pinch of salt

2 ripe Bursa figs, halved

110 g / 4 oz / ¾ cup raspberries

Method:

1. Pulse together the flour, butter, brown sugar, and salt in a food processor until the mixture resembles rough breadcrumbs.

2. Tip into two microwaveable mugs and add the figs and raspberries, tossing well to combine.

3. Microwave on high for 2 ½–3 minutes, rotating the mugs after 1 ½ minutes.

4. Remove from the microwave and leave to cool slightly before serving.

Banoffee Pudding Cups

PREPARATION TIME: 15 MINUTES

COOKING TIME: 5 MINUTES

Ingredients:

2 tbsp butter

75 g / 2 ½ oz / ⅓ cup soft light brown sugar

55 ml / 2 fl. oz / ¼ cup double (heavy) cream

a few drops of vanilla extract

2 small bananas, sliced

1 small egg white

a pinch of salt

a pinch of cream of tartar

1 tbsp caster (superfine) sugar

Method:

1. Divide the butter between two microwaveable cups, or a separate bowl (if using a bowl, transfer the caramel banana mixture to two cups after step 2).

2. Microwave on high for 30 seconds, or until melted. Carefully remove and divide the brown sugar and cream between the cups, stirring well to combine.

3. Microwave for a further 1–1 ½ minutes. Carefully remove, stir in the vanilla extract and microwave for a further 1 ½–2 minutes until golden and thickened. Remove to one side and fold through the bananas.

4. Beat the egg white with a pinch of salt and the cream of tartar in a clean bowl until softly peaked.

5. Combine the caster sugar with 1 tbsp of water in a small microwaveable mug. Cook on high for 30–40 seconds and stir. Continue to microwave in 10 second bursts until the syrup registers 116°C / 240F on a sugar thermometer.

6. Slowly beat the sugar syrup into the egg white until you have a thick, glossy meringue. Spoon the meringue into the cups and glaze with a chef's blowtorch before serving.

MAKES 4 MUGS

Rice Pudding with Cherry Compote

PREPARATION TIME: 5 MINUTES

COOKING TIME: 5 MINUTES

Ingredients:

200 g / 7 oz / 1 cup canned cherries in syrup

1 tbsp kirsch

1 tbsp lemon juice

110 g / 4 oz / ½ cup caster (superfine) sugar

500 ml / 18 fl. oz / 2 cups whole milk

½ tsp vanilla extract

300 g / 11 oz / 2 cups cooked short-grain rice

1 tsp ground cinnamon

Method:

1. Combine the cherries and syrup with the kirsch and lemon juice in a small microwaveable bowl. Cover with cling film and cook on high for 1 minute.

2. Carefully remove from the microwave and leave to cool to one side.

3. Combine the sugar, milk, and vanilla extract between four microwaveable mugs, stirring well to help dissolve the sugar. Cover with cling film and cook on medium for 2 minutes.

4. Carefully remove from the microwave and stir well. Divide the rice between the mugs, stir well and microwave on high for a further minute until the rice puddings are piping hot.

5. Garnish with the cherry compote and a generous pinch of ground cinnamon before serving.

Coffee Tiramisu

PREPARATION TIME: 15 MINUTES

Ingredients:

125 ml / 4 ½ fl. oz / ½ cup whipping cream, cold

125 g / 4 ½ oz / ½ cup mascarpone

2 tbsp caster (superfine) sugar

55 ml / 2 fl. oz / ¼ cup Marsala

8 savoiardi sponge fingers, chopped

110 ml / 4 fl. oz / ½ cup brewed coffee, cold

1 tbsp cocoa powder

1 tsp chocolate covered coffee beans

Method:

1. Whip together the cream, mascarpone, sugar and 1 tbsp of Marsala in a bowl until softly peaked and floppy.

2. Soak the sponge fingers in a mixture of coffee and the remaining Marsala. Position half of the soaked fingers in the base of two serving glasses or mugs.

3. Top with some of the whipped cream mixture and then top with the remaining soaked sponge fingers.

4. Spoon over the remaining cream mixture and top with a dusting of cocoa powder and a garnish of chocolate covered coffee beans.

5. Chill or serve immediately.

Quark Soufflé with Plums

PREPARATION TIME: 10 MINUTES

COOKING TIME: 5 MINUTES

Ingredients:

225 g / 8 oz / 1 cup quark

110 g / 4 oz / ½ cup honey

1 tsp vanilla extract

75 g / 3 oz / ½ cup plain (all-purpose) flour, sifted

½ tsp baking powder

4 medium eggs, separated

½ tsp cream of tartar

2 tbsp unsalted butter, softened

300 g / 10 ½ oz / 2 cups ripe plums, pitted and halved

2 tbsp caster (superfine) sugar, to garnish

Method:

1. Combine the quark, honey, vanilla extract, flour, baking powder and egg yolks in a large mixing bowl. Beat well until smooth, around 3 minutes.

2. Beat the egg whites with the cream of tartar in a separate, clean mixing bowl until stiffly peaked. Whisk one-third into the quark mixture and then cut and fold that mixture into the rest of the egg whites.

3. Grease four microwaveable mugs with the butter and fill with the soufflé batter. Stud with the plum halves.

4. Microwave on medium for 3–4 minutes, rotating the cups after 2 minutes, until the soufflés have risen to the lips of the mugs.

5. Carefully remove from the microwave and sprinkle with the sugar before serving.

Malva Pudding

PREPARATION TIME: 15 MINUTES

COOKING TIME: 5 MINUTES

Ingredients:

1 tbsp sunflower oil

275 g / 10 oz / 1 ¼ cups caster (superfine) sugar

2 large eggs

2 tbsp apricot jam (jelly)

75 g / 3 oz / ⅓ cup unsalted butter, melted

1 tsp distilled vinegar

75 ml / 3 fl. oz / ⅓ cup whole milk

150 g / 5 oz / 1 cup plain (all-purpose) flour, sifted

1 tsp baking powder

a pinch of salt

250 ml / 9 fl. oz / 1 cup double (heavy) cream

2 tsp vanilla extract

Method:

1. Grease four large microwaveable mugs with sunflower oil.

2. Beat together 175 g / 6 oz / ¾ cup sugar with the eggs in a large mixing bowl using an electric mixer. Once pale and thick, add the apricot jam and beat again for a further minute.

3. Add 1 tbsp of melted butter as well as the vinegar and milk. Beat briefly and then fold through the flour, baking powder and salt until combined.

4. Divide the batter between the mugs and cook in the microwave on medium for 2 minutes. Test with a toothpick; if it comes out clean, the puddings are done. If not, cook at 15-second intervals until done. Carefully remove to a wire rack to cool, pricking each pudding several times with a toothpick.

5. Combine the remaining sugar and butter with the cream, 75 ml / 3 fl. oz / ⅓ cup of water and vanilla extract in a microwaveable bowl. Microwave on high for 2 minutes, stirring after 1 minute. Leave to cool and thicken slightly before pouring over the puddings and serving.

Strawberry Jelly Cups

PREPARATION TIME: 5 MINUTES

COOKING TIME: 2 MINUTES   **CHILLING TIME:** 4 HOURS

Ingredients:

35 g / 1 ½ oz / ¼ cup strawberry jelly (gelatin mixture), cubed

125 ml / 4 ½ fl. oz / ½ cup hot water

Method:

1. Divide the cubed jelly and hot water between two microwaveable mugs. Stir briefly and then microwave on high in 10-second intervals, stirring after each, until the jelly has dissolved.

2. Top up with a little cold water and then cover and chill for 4 hours until set.

3. Serve straight from the fridge.

Egg Custard Mug

PREPARATION TIME: 10 MINUTES

COOKING TIME: 10 MINUTES

Ingredients:

450 ml / 16 fl. oz / 2 cups whole milk

55 g / 2 oz / ¼ cup caster (superfine) sugar

4 medium egg yolks

½ tsp vanilla extract

2 tbsp milk chocolate

1 tsp fresh nutmeg

Method:

1. Divide the milk and sugar between four large microwaveable mugs. Microwave on high for 3–4 minutes, stirring every minute, until the sugar has dissolved and small bubbles form at the edges of the milk.

2. Gently beat an egg yolk and a few drops of vanilla extract into each mug. Cook in the microwave on medium for 3–4 minutes, whisking every minute, until thickened.

3. Carefully remove from the microwave and leave to cool slightly for 5 minutes. Grate over some chocolate and fresh nutmeg before serving.

Berry and Almond Brioche Bake

PREPARATION TIME: 5–10 MINUTES

COOKING TIME: 1–2 MINUTES

Ingredients:

1 tsp unsalted butter, melted

1 small egg, beaten

a few drops of vanilla extract

110 g / 4 oz brioche loaf, cut into pieces

55 g / 2 oz / ½ cup blueberries

1 tbsp flaked (slivered) almonds

1 tsp caster (superfine) sugar

Method:

1. Butter the insides of a large, microwaveable mug with the melted butter.

2. Beat the egg with the vanilla extract. Soak the brioche in the egg and arrange in the mug, adding some of the blueberries and almonds between pieces.

3. Top with the remaining blueberries and almonds and microwave on medium for 30–60 seconds.

4. Carefully remove from the microwave and top with the sugar. Return to the microwave and cook for a further 15 seconds before serving.

Orange and Caramel Soufflé Bake

PREPARATION TIME: 15 MINUTES

COOKING TIME: 10 MINUTES

Ingredients:

3 large eggs, separated

2 tbsp granulated sugar

75 ml / 3 fl. oz / ⅓ cup whole milk

2 tbsp plain (all-purpose) flour

1 tbsp orange zest

2 tbsp triple sec

2 tbsp unsalted butter, melted

75 g / 3 oz / ⅓ cup caster (superfine) sugar

2 tbsp water

1 orange, segmented

Method:

1. Beat the egg whites with the granulated sugar in a clean mixing bowl until stiffly peaked.

2. Beat together the egg yolks, milk, flour, orange zest, and **triple sec** in a separate mixing bowl until smooth. Whisk one third of the egg whites into the egg yolk mixture and then fold through the remaining egg whites.

3. Grease four microwaveable mugs with the butter and then divide the batter between the mugs. Chill until ready to cook.

4. Stir together the caster sugar and water in a microwaveable jug. Cook in the microwave on high for 1 minute. Remove, stir and continue to microwave in 10-second increments until an amber caramel forms.

5. Microwave the soufflés on high in 30-second increments until they are risen above the rim of the mugs. Remove from the microwave and serve with the caramel and orange segments on top.

CAKE IN A MUG

Chocolate Mug Cake

PREPARATION TIME: 5 MINUTES

COOKING TIME: 10 MINUTES

Ingredients:

110 g / 4 oz / ½ cup margarine, softened

110 g / 4 oz / ½ cup caster (superfine) sugar

100 g / 3 ½ oz / ⅔ cup self-raising flour

2 tbsp cocoa powder

2 large eggs

1 tbsp whole milk

150 g / 5 oz / 1 cup dark chocolate

75 ml / 3 fl. oz / ⅓ cup double (heavy) cream

Method:

1. Divide the margarine, sugar, flour, cocoa powder, eggs and milk between four microwaveable mugs and mix until combined.

2. Cover with cling film, then poke a few holes in the cling film and microwave the cakes for 1 minute.

3. Carefully remove from the microwave and test with a wooden toothpick; it it comes out clean, they are ready. If not, continue to cook in 15-second bursts until done.

4. Chop most of the chocolate and set it to one side. Curl the remainder using a cheese slice.

5. Place the cream in a microwaveable bowl and microwave on high for 1 minute until hot. Add the chocolate, leave to stand for 30 seconds, then stir until smooth.

6. Spoon over the cakes and then garnish with the curled chocolate on top.

MAKES
4
MUGS

Chocolate Panettone

PREPARATION TIME: 10 MINUTES
COOKING TIME: 2 MINUTES

Ingredients:

2 tbsp butter, melted

1 medium egg

50 g / 1 ¾ oz / ⅓ cup strong plain (all-purpose) flour

a pinch of baking powder

½ tsp dried active yeast

a pinch of caster (superfine) sugar

a pinch of salt

75 g / 2 ½ oz / ½ cup dark chocolate chips

1 tsp icing (confectioners') sugar

Method:

1. Combine the butter, eggs, flour, baking powder, yeast, sugar and salt in a mixing bowl. Mix well until a rough dough comes together.

2. Add the chocolate chips and mix well to incorporate, kneading briefly.

3. Shape the dough into two microwaveable mugs and microwave on medium for 1 ½ minutes, checking after 1 minute, or until risen. Once risen, remove to a wire rack to cool.

4. Garnish with a dusting of icing sugar before serving.

Mocha Cake

PREPARATION TIME: 10 MINUTES

COOKING TIME: 5 MINUTES

Ingredients:

110 g / 4 oz / ½ cup butter, melted

110 g / 4 oz / ½ cup soft light brown sugar

100 g / 3 ½ oz / ⅔ cup self-raising flour

55 g / 2 oz / ½ cup cocoa powder

2 tbsp whole milk

1 tsp instant espresso, dissolved in 1 tbsp boiling water

chocolate sauce, to serve

2 tbsp icing (confectioners') sugar

Method:

1. Divide the melted butter, brown sugar, flour, cocoa powder, milk and espresso between four microwaveable mugs, mixing until combined.

2. Cover with cling film, poking a few holes in it, then cook on high for 1 minute.

3. Carefully remove from the microwave and test using a wooden toothpick; if it comes out clean, the cakes are done. If not, continue to cook in 10-second bursts until ready.

4. Remove the cling film, top with chocolate sauce and dust with icing sugar before serving.

Gooey Coffee Cake

PREPARATION TIME: 5 MINUTES

COOKING TIME: 1–2 MINUTES

Ingredients:

55 g / 2 oz / ¼ cup unsalted butter, melted

55 g / 2 oz / ¼ cup soft light brown sugar

50 g / 1 ¾ oz / ⅓ cup self-raising flour, sifted

1 tsp cornflour (cornstarch)

1 large egg, beaten

1 tsp instant espresso, dissolved in 1 tbsp boiling water

4 mini chocolate and vanilla sandwich cookies

1 tsp icing (confectioners') sugar

Method:

1. Divide the melted butter, sugar, flour, cornflour, egg and espresso between two microwaveable mugs, beating to combine.

2. Cover with cling film and poke a few holes in it, then cook on medium for 30–60 seconds.

3. Carefully remove and check; if a wooden toothpick comes out almost clean, they are done. If not, continue to microwave in 10-second increments until ready.

4. Serve the mug cakes with a couple of the mini cookies on top and a light dusting of icing sugar.

Sticky Caramel Mug Cake

PREPARATION TIME: 10 MINUTES

COOKING TIME: 5 MINUTES

Ingredients:

150 ml / 5 fl. oz / ⅔ cup double (heavy) cream

100 g / 3 ½ oz / ⅓ cup golden syrup

2 tbsp soft light brown sugar

2 tbsp unsalted butter

110 g / 4 oz / ½ cup margarine, softened

110 g / 4 oz / ½ cup caster (superfine) sugar

110 g / 4 oz / ⅔ cup self-raising flour

2 large eggs

1 tsp vanilla extract

Method:

1. Combine the cream, golden syrup, brown sugar and butter in a microwaveable jug or bowl. Microwave on high for 2 minutes, stirring after 1 minute, until golden in appearance.

2. Divide half of the sauce between four microwaveable mugs. Set the remainder to one side.

3. Beat together the remaining ingredients in a large mixing bowl until smooth. Spoon the batter on top of the sauce in the mugs. Cover with cling film, poking a few holes in the cling film.

4. Microwave on high for 1 minute. If toothpick comes out clean, the cakes are done. If not, continue to microwave in 10-second increments until done.

5. When ready, spoon over the remaining sauce before serving.

MAKES
4
MUGS

Mint Cupcakes

PREPARATION TIME: 15 MINUTES

COOKING TIME: 5 MINUTES

Ingredients:

110 g / 4 oz / ½ cup margarine, softened

110 g / 4 oz / ⅔ cup self-raising flour, sifted

110 g / 4 oz / ½ cup caster (superfine) sugar

2 large eggs

1 ½ tsp peppermint extract

55 g / 2 oz / ⅓ cup chocolate chunks

150 g / 5 oz / ⅔ cup unsalted butter, softened

175 g / 6 oz / 1 ½ cups icing (confectioners') sugar, sifted

1 tbsp double (heavy) cream

4 mint chocolate squares, halved

Method:

1. Divide the margarine, flour, caster sugar, eggs and 1 tsp of the peppermint extract between four microwaveable mugs, beating until smooth.

2. Stud the top with a few chocolate chunks and cover the mugs with cling film, poking a few holes.

3. Cook on high for 1 minute. If a wooden toothpick comes out clean, the cakes are ready. If not, continue to microwave in 10-second increments until ready.

4. Carefully remove the cupcakes to a wire rack to cool. Beat together the butter, icing sugar, cream and remaining peppermint extract in a mixing bowl until pale and creamy.

5. Spoon into a piping bag fitted with a star-shaped nozzle. Pipe swirls of the buttercream on top of the cupcakes and garnish with the halved chocolate squares before serving.

121

Summer Fruit Mug Cake

PREPARATION TIME: 5 MINUTES

COOKING TIME: 2 MINUTES

Ingredients:

2 tbsp butter

2 tbsp caster (superfine) sugar

2 tbsp self-raising flour

1 medium egg

1 tbsp milk

2 tbsp frozen mixed berries (defrosted)

1 tbsp strawberry jam (jelly)

Method:

1. Mix the butter and sugar in a large, microwaveable mug, then add the egg and stir until combined.

2. Gradually stir in the flour, then add the milk and mix well. Fold in 1 tbsp of the mixed berries.

3. Cover the mug with cling film, poking a few holes in the cling film. Place the mug in the centre of the microwave and cook for 1 ½ minutes until well risen; if a wooden toothpick comes out clean, the cakes are done. If not, continue to microwave in 10-second increments until ready.

4. In a separate mug, combine the remaining frozen berries and jam, then microwave for 30 seconds. Spoon the cooked berries onto the cake and serve.

Blueberry Cake

PREPARATION TIME: 20 MINUTES

COOKING TIME: 5 MINUTES

Ingredients:

150 g / 5 ¼ oz / 1 ¼ cups blueberries

55 g / 2 oz / ¼ cup margarine, softened

55 g / 2 oz / ¼ cup golden caster (superfine) sugar

55 g / 2 oz / ⅓ cup self-raising flour

a pinch of bicarbonate of (baking) soda

1 large egg, beaten

75 ml / 2 ½ fl. oz / ⅓ cup double (heavy) cream

1 tbsp icing (confectioners') sugar

a pinch of freeze-dried blueberry powder

Method:

1. Combine 50 g / 1 ½ oz / ⅓ cup of blueberries with the margarine, caster sugar, flour, bicarbonate of soda and eggs in a food processor. Blitz until smooth, then divide the batter between two microwaveable mugs.

2. Cover the mugs with cling film, poking a few holes in the cling film. Microwave on high for 45–60 seconds. then check; if a wooden toothpick comes out clean, the cakes are done. If not, continue to microwave in 10-second increments until ready.

3. Carefully remove to a wire rack to cool. Blitz half of the remaining blueberries in a clean food processor until puréed. Pass the purée through a fine sieve into a bowl.

4. Whip the cream with the icing sugar in a separate bowl until softly peaked. Fold the blueberry purée through the cream and spoon it into a piping bag fitted with a small, star-shaped nozzle.

5. Pipe the cream on top of the cakes and garnish with the blueberry powder and remaining blueberries before serving.

INDEX